AF481077

THE BEGINNING AND END OF THE GREAT DEPRESSION

US HISTORY LEADING TO GREAT DEPRESSION

Children's American History of 1900s

During the 1930s, there was an economic crisis which came to be known as the Great Depression. It started in the United States but ended up spreading throughout the world.

People were unemployed, homeless, and hungry. In this book, you will be learning about the beginning and the end of the Great Depression.

WHAT CAUSED THE GREAT DEPRESSION?

It was not a single factor or event that caused it. There were many conditions taking place at one time which made the economy go downhill.

MIGRANT MOTHER WITH HER KIDS

THE STOCK MARKET CRASH

The Stock Market Crash, occurring in 1929, is usually known to be the start of the Great Depression. The market had crashed because of "over speculation". That occurs when once stocks are worth more than the company's real value. People had started using credit obtained from banks to buy stock, but this rise in the stock market was not based on reality.

S tocks then began to fall once the economy started to slow. During October of 1929, people started to panic and started to sell their stocks. This caused the market to crash and many lost everything. While this was not the only factor causing the Great Depression, it most likely got it started.

CROWD OF EXCITED TRADERS
AT STOCK EXCHANGE, 1920'S

UNEMPLOYED MEN QUEUED OUTSIDE A DEPRESSION SOUP KITCHEN

This became known as one of the most horrific stock market crashes during the history of the U.S. Value of the stocks started falling dramatically during the next several days towards the end of October. People had lost their savings and were now losing their homes as well. Businesses were having to lay off employees and go bankrupt. The stock market crash became the signal for the beginning of the Great Depression that ended up last over ten years.

BEFORE THE CRASH

Also known as the Roaring Twenties, the 1920s had become a time of business speculation and economic boom. New industries, including radios and autos, were changing America culture.

A FLAPPER AND GRAMOPHONE,
EARLY 1920'S

P eople believed everyone was now going to be wealthy and had faith that their economy was not going to stop growing.

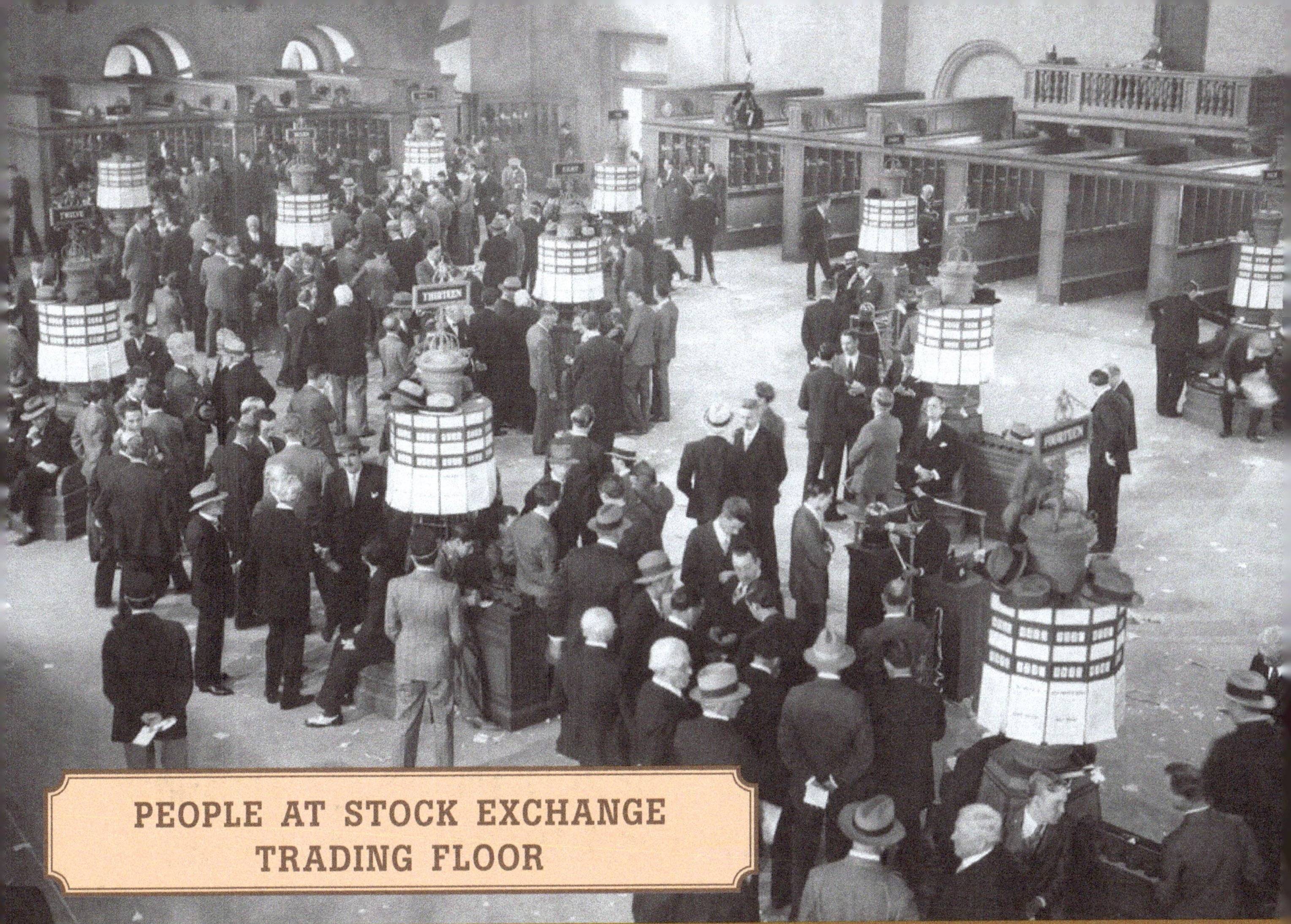

PEOPLE AT STOCK EXCHANGE TRADING FLOOR

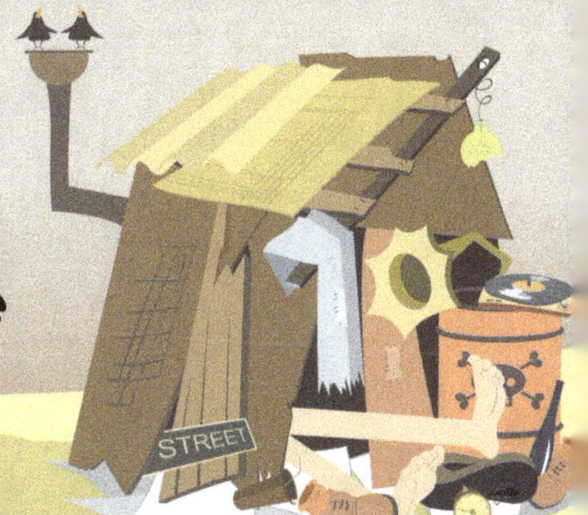

This caused great speculation in the stock market and between 1921 and 1929 the market was up by 600% and the Dow Jones Industrial Average rose from 63 to 381 points.

THE CRASH

However, the stock market's crazy rise was not based on reality since the economy couldn't grow at this rate forever. The economy started its downfall in 1929. Panic took over in October, and people started selling huge amounts of their stock. October 28th and October 29th were the worst days, as values went down 23% and were referred to as "Black Monday" and "Black Tuesday".

BOARD AT THE TORONTO STOCK EXCHANGE

33569.36
25.10 -1.5 9356.63 6.99 11.52 10520.39
58.55 33569.36 369.66 36.58
800.52 36.45 + 120.36 4.89
3655.89 50089.30 120.36 2554.01 31.33
1345.00 56.58 94.01 6.99 38.78 45.12
5654.89 456.99 32554.0 6359.36
20.36 -3.65 89.00 +1.33
+ 120.36
+1.33
281.53 -9.10 +1.32 4033.15 25.56
-2.25 -1.5 563.39
19346.95 28.31 -3.58 65.52 +1.52
800.33 -0.52 23155.58 800.5
2.25 659.10 931456.95
5.34 565.34 358.85
1043.35 -95.46

Even though it tried to rally, the market was not able to recover and over the next few months, it fell about 40%, with many losing all they had. During the summer of 1932, the market had dropped 89%. Billions had been eradicated and the U.S. was now in a deep economic depression.

During most of the 1920s, farmers were struggling, even prior to the Great Depression. They had new machinery and were able to grow more crops than they had before. This, however, caused prices to drop too low and they were not able to see a profit.

Things got worse once the Great Depression struck. A drought had started in the Midwest that lasted through 1939 and their soil turned to dust.

Farmers were not able to pay the bills and ended up losing their farms. They proceeded to migrate to California looking for work.

PEOPLE BORROWED TOO MUCH MONEY

During the 1920s, there were many new products such as washing machines, autos, and radios. Advertising had convinced them that they could borrow money and afford to purchase these items. Many people incurred debt to buy products that they could not afford. Once the economy went downhill, many were not able to make these payments.

120
THE SATURDAY EVENING POST
December 4, 192
Westinghouse
ELECTRIC WARE FOR CHRISTMAS GIFTS
Send a Package
of Convenience
Westinghouse Electric Ware is a truly convenient Christmas gift—convenient not only to use but also to give. Since Westinghouse appliances are alike in beauty and utility wherever you find them, they may be ordered by mail or 'phone from any Westinghouse dealer with entire assurance. Moreover, each piece comes all packaged for shipment. Those who must buy hurriedly will find these facts worth remembering.
Single pieces of Westinghouse Ware are often tasteful gifts for an entire family. This but adds to their suitability as remembrances for individuals. Such are the
TURNOVER TOASTER
TOASTER STOVE   PERCOLATOR
Or you can select from a list that includes
"THE IRON THAT WOMEN DESIGNED"
TRAVELER'S IRON   COZY GLOW
CURLING IRON   WARMING PAD
In the kitchen, convenience has been given a new significance by the "Westinghouse Automatic Range." There is no finer year 'round gift for the whole family.
These all await your convenience at the nearest Westinghouse store.
WESTINGHOUSE ELECTRIC & MANUFACTURING CO.
W
WESTINGHOUSE ELECTRIC
Westinghouse
Turnover T
Westinghouse
Electric Coffee Percolator

FACTORY WORKERS 1920

TOO MANY GOODS

Economy had started booming during the 1920s and companies constructed new factories and hired additional workers. Companies were soon making more products than what they could sell.

Once the Depression began, companies were now having to halt production and lay off workers, which had a negative effect to the economy.

U.S. BANK BUILDING PORTLAND
OREGON 1920

A major factor leading to the Great Depression was collapse of the banking system. During the first years of the Great Depression, over 10,000 banks had failed and many had lost their total savings. Several went from being wealthy to not having anything at all. The government of the United States was doing little to assist the banks.

Economy around the world was now struggling. The United States had loaned money to their allies that were recuperating from WWI. While these countries were also struggling, they were unable to pay the back the borrowed money to the United States.

SMOOT AND HAWLEY STANDING TOGETHER

n 1930, there was a law named the Smoot-Hawley Tariff Act passed which placed high taxes (tariffs) on imports and this stalled trade with other countries which also helped in slowing the economy.

WAS THE PRESIDENT TO BLAME?

At the start of the Great Depression, Herbert Hoover had been President of the United States and many blamed him for it. There were shantytowns for the homeless to live called "Hoovervilles", named after him. Franklin Roosevelt was elected President of the United States in 1933 and promised a "New Deal" for America.

HERBERT CLARK HOOVER

FIGHTER PLANES DURING WORLD WAR 2

WHEN DID THE GREAT DEPRESSION END?

Just like it didn't start in one day, it also did not end in just one day and all was better. The exact date is debated by economists as well as historians. Most people believe that the "start of the end" was in 1939, at the start of World War II.

WHAT WAS THE REASON FOR THE END OF THE GREAT DEPRESSION?

The cause of the end of the Great Depression is also debated by many historians, most believe it was World War II. Once the war started, factories had returned to full production to build supplies for war including airplanes, tanks, guns, ammo, and ships.

WOMEN ALUMINUM SHELLS WWII

U nemployment was dropping was young men were now joining the army and people were going to work in the factories. Others believe it was the New Deal laws that brought the end.

There is no doubt that many factors helped in getting the economy of the United States going. Government regulations, World War II, the end of the drought in the Midwest, and a new system of banking all were factors contributing to the rise of the economy.

A lasting legacy remained on the government and the people of the United States as a result of the Great Depression. Many that had lived through this time period now had no faith in the banking systems and would no longer use credit to purchase goods.

BANKING
DATA
downloading 70% C
35%
25%
25%
10%
5%
89%

Their purchases were made using cash and they would store emergency rations.

Others believed that the depression had made them stronger, as well as their country. People had learned about hard work as well as how to survive.

WAS ABOUT THE NEW DEAL?

There were several laws and agencies that were created under the New Deal that would change the United States forever. It changed the way citizens felt about the roles of government. The Social Security Act was probably the most important of these new laws. It provided, through payroll tax, retirement for the country's elderly, assistance for the disabled, and insurance for the unemployed. These laws still play a major role in today's government.

SOCIAL SECURITY

EXTERIOR OF FEDERAL DEPOSIT INSURANCE CORPORATION BUILDING IN ARLINGTON, VA

O ther programs included in the New Deal that still impact our lives are banking reform (such as the FDIC insurance that keeps money you have at the bank safe), regulations regarding the stock market (keeping companies from lying about profits), housing and farm programs, and laws to protect and regulate unions.

The public works programs, including the PWA, the CCC, and WPA, did more than only providing jobs for people that were unemployed, they would end up leaving a long-lasting mark on the United States.

WOMEN WORKING FOR THE WPA

T he Works Progress Administration (WPA) built more than 8,000 parks, 5,000 schools, 1,000 libraries, and more than 650,000 miles of new roads, as well as repairing or constructing more

WPA POSTER WORKSHOP

than 124,000 bridges. Several of these parks, libraries, schools, roads, and bridges continue to be used today.

HERBERT HOOVER

Herbert Hoover was the 31st President of the U.S. and served from 1929 to 1933. He is best known for serving as president in 1929, at the time of the stock market crash that people believe was the start of the Great Depression.

PRESIDENT FRANKLIN D. ROOSEVELT

Franklin D. Roosevelt was the 32nd President of the U.S. and served from 1933 to 1945. He is best known for leading the U.S. along with the Allied Powers against Germany and Japan's Axis powers during WWII.

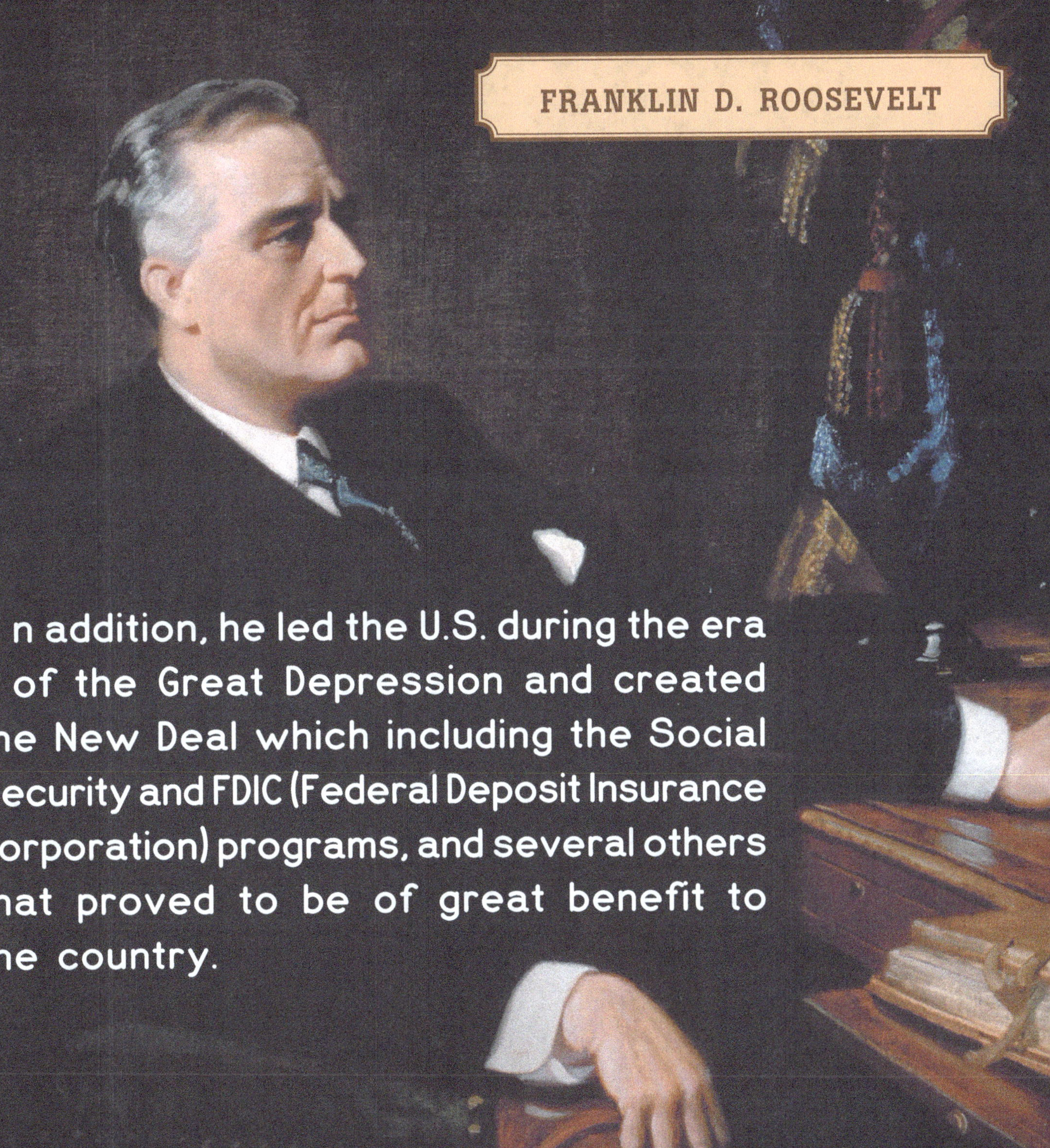

In addition, he led the U.S. during the era of the Great Depression and created the New Deal which including the Social Security and FDIC (Federal Deposit Insurance Corporation) programs, and several others that proved to be of great benefit to the country.

SCHOOLCHILDREN LINE UP FOR
FREE ISSUE OF SOUP AND A SLICE OF
BREAD IN THE DEPRESSION

The Great Depression was a time of horrible struggle for many people throughout the world. There were several causes for the start of it, as well as many events that brought it to an end. Today, we still enjoy some of the results of the New Deal, which may not have happened if it weren't for the Great Depression. For additional information about the Great Depression, you can visit the local library, research the internet, and ask questions of your teachers, family, and friends.

Visit
BABY PROFESSOR
EDUCATION KIDS
www.BabyProfessorBooks.com
to download Free Baby Professor eBooks
and view our catalog of new and exciting
Children's Books